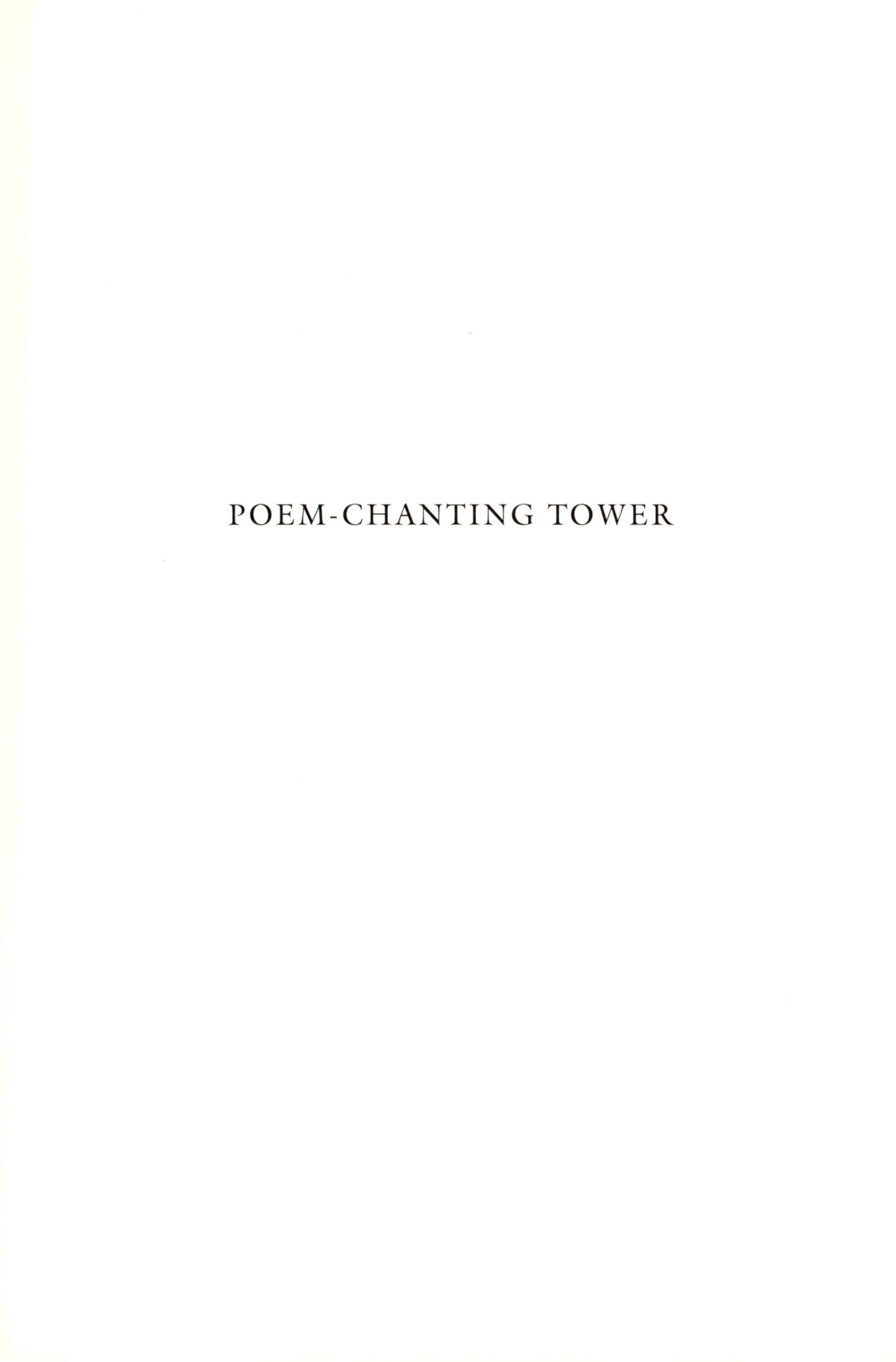

POEM-CHANTING TOWER

POEM-CHANTING TOWER

A Tribute to Xue Tao

WILLIAM HOLLIS

*William Hollis
19 Dec 01*

*Dear Alexa & Fred —
May your holidays
be full of richness
and love —
Bill*

HAWKHURST BOOKS

Copyright ® 2007 by William Hollis
ISBN 978-0-9748304-1-4
Hawkhurst Books, 6122 Butler Pike, Blue Bell, PA 19422
www.williamhollis.com

'Poem of Autumn'
by Wen Cheng-ming (1470-1559)
is reproduced with permission of the Philadelphia Museum of Art
(photo by Graydon Wood, 2007)

AUTHOR'S NOTE

'Poem-Chanting Tower' was the name of the house that Xue Tao, courtesan and poet, built at her retirement in 810 A.D. on the banks of the Brocade River, just a few hundred yards downriver from the house of Tu Fu, China's most famous poet.

The poems in this volume gathered words slowly over a quarter of a century even as they looked back to Xue Tao's 9th century or to my years in Vermont or to more recent years when I decided to encounter more vividly an ancient world where I wake at night and find myself.

Felice Fischer, curator and friend, showed me original images and academic translations of Wen Cheng-ming's fan and the panels by Nukina Kaioku, Wang Hsi-chi's 'At the Orchid Pavilion' and Tu Fu's 'Eight Famous Drinkers' and 'Afternoon on the Brocade River.'

I hope she will not be disappointed with how I have ripped and restructured.

CONTENTS

Author's Note / 5
Contents / 7

After Reading T'ang Poetry / 9
Farewell and Welcome / 10
Brief Lyrics for Ancient Chinese Friends / 14
In the Studio / 17

Belated Tributes / 18
That Face at the Bar / 21
For Old Meng / 22
An Apprentice at the Lute / 25

Poem-Chanting Tower / 26
A Little Touch of Truth / 30
A Dance at the Shrine / 33
Portrait / 34

Encounter in the Garden / 36
Brushing Cold Fishing Nets / 38
Young Painter / 40
Death and the Poet / 42

The Last Voyage / 44
Dragon Robe / 48
Waiting / 51
Letter from Exile / 52

Dying Flowers for Xue Tao / 53
Twelve Mornings / 54
Landscape of the Heart / 56
Tu Fu's Voyage of Farewell / 62

Afternoon on the Brocade River / 74
Eight Famous Drinkers / 76
Orchid Pavilion / 78
Chinese Scholar's Study / 81

Dream Lanterns / 84
Autumn Comes / 86
Ten Conveniences / 88
For Ts'ang Chieh / 93

Cold-Mountain Poems / 94
Buddha's Sermon at Lu Zhai / 96

Translation of Fan / 98
Biographical Note / 100
Books by William Hollis / 102

/ 7

AFTER READING T'ANG POETRY

I could wish for a year
in which one might speak of poems
as 'brief fragments of a soul's music'
in which one might say to a poet
'you give tongue to the tongue
that cleaves to the roof of my palate'

I could wish for that summer
high in the mountains above Ch'ang-an
when an emperor might envy
a distant garden
a clarity of light
and a brush that moves with the wind
across white silk

but it is dusty
here above the city
at night angry voices push at my curtains
at dawn eager alarms scrape
at the soft light
and poke at piles of rubbish
intruding dark corners of the alley

half awake
I dream of another season
and the soft stepping of deer
when I would send for your response
this verse
this brief fragment
an unresolved music that echoes still
above the surface of this page

FAREWELL AND WELCOME

I

for Yau Ywe-hwa

six poems was all
six poems
and then you sailed away into the night
down a river
down a way I could not go

you sent me six poems at midnight
but at dawn
the current was swifter
where your father's boat rose and fell
with the tide

I have read aloud your poems
each day for twenty years
I call out
to each silken ship that passes
'have you seen the woman
who wrote six poems of farewell'

I have only these poems
these brief songs
when I raise them to my lips
your fragrance lingers
across the swift dark tide

II

for Madame Meng

a thousand years ago
you heard the lute
jade fingers on strings the color of blood
and for a thousand years
we've heard your cry

and only today
touching a note
at the bottom of the page
did I know that only two survive
two poems
that's all

you burned the rest
and turned and said
it was not proper for a woman to shine

silk should fall from arms
not carry the weight of words

I write across the years
seeking your voice
again and again
inviting you to be heard
to play your lute
through space that intervenes

III

for Li Ching-jau

during the autumn festival
we climbed to the top of Hubbard Hill
and wrote poetry by moonlight
or was it only that we drank too much wine

do you remember

I finished fifteen lyrics
beside the one
that took you the whole night
as you chewed your tongue
and the tip of your brush

at dawn
when we hung the scrolls at the gate
early wanderers
pausing in preparation for the day
gathered to murmur gratitude
before that one quiet song

did I ever acknowledge those lines
that moved so beautifully down the page

each autumn
I stumble on another scroll
a bowl
a comb you left behind

IV

my sisters my lovers
there on the Yangtze River
the Ompompanusic
yesterday
when the flood tide ran to the sea
I thought of you
and a life shorter than this poem

if I sit very still and listen
I can hear
under moonlight
the soft tracking of your brush
and a whisper in the shadows
almost a singing

I cannot be silent
under the fall of your voices
there is a song
that scratches at my throat
that trespasses
the slippery steps of this house

when I pull back the curtains
there is no one there
only on silk
or a thin sheet of smeared paper
can I know the syllables
of your sad renunciation

BRIEF LYRICS
FOR ANCIENT CHINESE FRIENDS

I

I write neither on silk
nor with a brush
push instead at keys
and watch the whirring chop of letters
as they mark their hesitant progress

if you could hear me whisper these lines
that move in a contrary direction
that linger here on the page
would you recognize an old friend

is it presumptuous
to hint at love
to swear I've known you
these thousand years

it was only yesterday
I found another of your scrolls

II

your lives differ
from those I've imagined

the captain's daughter
found to her chagrin
her scholar/poet was bald
and had bad breath

and Madame Meng knew
that climbing mountains
moved her more than verse
and so she burnt the poems
and sighed in her relief
embittered and alone

nor was it Li
who died before her husband
for twenty years indulging a memory
she brushed a history
of grief
an echo of desire

III

is it too much to say
I hear the pitch of your voice
here
further from the court of Ch'ang-an
than the most distant branch of the Yangtze

if these ancient letters
that hang beside my door
are nothing more than signs
for a rag and bone shop
they carry still
the ease and flow of your brush

if it is a dream
a restless tossing at midnight
it is at least
how the heart lies within itself
imagining your voice
and the movement of your life

IN THE STUDIO

among debris and dust
the shriveled gloves her mother wore
a box of yellow teeth
glittering virgins from a sunnier place
and scrawled quotations from a favored poet
she piles the heads her fingers make
her heart has seen
her nightmares give

she smiles and smiles
and piles the bones about the heads
with teeth her uncle left
with dreams and angry tears
with all those withered faces
grimaced in glass
with memories reflected from the case
with footsteps dying down the corridor

she piles the heads
beside a photograph her daughter sent
and smiles at a fist of clay
and lets her fingers push at eyes
'you can not see behind their dusty glass
you only see your dusty face'
it all begins and ends among debris
among the boxes full of time and tears

BELATED TRIBUTES

I

during the long evening
she stands on the deck absorbed in a mystery
deeper than tides

lamps glitter
two or three reflected and fractured
until the river swarms with golden butterflies

the wind lifts her gown
pulls it taut against the light
leaves me breathless
at the thin stillness of her body
a calligraphic mark against the light
a deliberate pressure from a brush

I hold my breath
and pull my own brush
down a length of unresistant silk

I am afraid that if I blink and look again
the wind will swirl
empty
where she had stood

II

the music is too loud in the small room
I can hear
neither the urgent whisper from the next table
nor that insistent music

as for her voice
I have already lost it

surely she sang a song of lost love
but I can hear only a hum
in the lull following a cadence
a harsh regret for lost sleep

even the scratch of my brush
a worn brush almost ready for discarding
adds its thin sound
to the crescendo of this room

a door slams
an accent to voices that rise
and push at the music

my notebook skids across the table
splashes the wine

and her voice
the very memory of her voice
fades even from the voicing of these syllables

III

she leaves at midnight
and for a long time afterwards
I can hear only her trotting horse
or is it the splash of her oars
as she slips to the tide

later
as silence takes hold of my sails
there is a call of geese
as they fly on
brief marks of the brush against an autumn moon

at dawn
awake and refusing to weep
I hear again the fading call of geese
on and on
into some distant forgetfulness

I would like to imagine
a gathering of tears
in this ancient small jar the color of blood
but it is only water to wash out the ink

THAT FACE AT THE BAR

a thousand years ago she sat at the same bar
the same pout and shadow at the eye
'but why'
I said then
as now someone else whispers ungently
a high flush at the slow realization
of the distance of flesh

a thousand years without stillness
and I am still provoked
by that face that closes inward
against the crush of the afternoon

I almost rise and call
but a thousand years is too great a distance
I am held in my chair
by more than this heavy flesh
this stiffness of the spine

it is she and not she
not she alone
but all the unanswering faces
against whom I have whispered
with more urgency than sense
'but why... why'

and it is I and not I
not I alone
who sits here in the afternoon
watching lovely faces that turn inward
that close against the world

FOR OLD MENG

I

the boniness of your verse
the anger in a voice that will not stay still
the jagged knocking of elbows and knees
no wonder the women of the court giggled
and hid their eyes
in the drape of silver sleeves

you said it was a matter of honesty
a deal you made
with frogs in a stagnant pond
'let them sing to please a sated queen'
you said
though when you turned and left the room
there was a plop and splash
in the uneasy silence

II

I had not known
had thought it was just your way
a lifetime of anger

I should have known
should have guessed

last week's roses wilted at the first touch
two perfect buds
by noon the petals had fallen and curled
scratching at the table
like tiny brown fingers

before I lit the lamp
I brushed away their dust

I should have pulled out the old vines
let in the air
opened roots to the rain

ah yes
I should have known

III

I turned from wild imprecisions
of your thought
to brush music across this page

I did not notice the dimming light
until the sun
at a moment of slipping
from clouds to the earth
washed out the unfinished page
with a cast of gold

it is dark at the desk
where I no longer write

was it you who turned out the lamp
who whipped your anger from river to river
who died a thousand years ago

you left those poems
which even now
remembered
leave me breathless
as I push through the dark corridor

AN APPRENTICE AT THE LUTE

there is a rustle of dismay
when she appears
a moody angry child
who glowers
and seems to resist the evening's play

but when her fingers touch the strings
music spills with energy
elegant and glittering
with inner voices never heard
until this pouring of notes
this precision
this irrepressible sweep and flow

I hold my breath
sit forward
lean against onrushing sound
hear only the sound
wrapped within

and forget the child
until
with petulance
a glare and a shrug
she finishes
and rushes from the room

POEM-CHANTING TOWER

A Presentation for Xue Tao

I

I can not imagine the years
when generals sat smiling at your song
or scholars came a great distance
to ask a favor

years later
when it was no longer necessary
for you to rise in the middle of the night
to comfort an official
dropped by the latest turn of government
I stood watching
from the shadow of an arbor
as you sat in the sun
and brushed poems
on slips of bright paper

and I was there
when young poets brought scrolls
with small perfect poems
though I was not among the pretty ones
who played golden lutes
but a gray one
with breath too short to finish a line

when you came close and listened
the very air trembled
and lilies burst open
with a shudder
and flooded the garden with perfume
as rich and haunting as the musk
in the scarf you wound about my shoulders

I keep it still
in a box with these poems
that were for you

when all the world was a landscape
fading from the scroll that hung in a corner
lit only by the turning of the stars

2

after the emissaries had left
tall strangers
with red hair
who came from beyond the mountains
to see for themselves
a woman who had brushed more eloquently
than any man

after they had mounted their horses
amid a clatter of drums
and the shrill sounding of flutes
and there was again silence in the courtyard
and dust settled
and birds sang again in the garden

after such tribute
after such a stir on the banks of the river
how can you see these inadequate words
that leave a slight trail of ink
as the brush lifts
and moves on

how can you hear the suppressed song
that centers time
on this white expanse
how can you know what I feel
as I wait here
at the end of the corridor
where morning sun
bright across the sheen of this paper
pushes back at my brush

3

I do not remember when it happened
a time of illness
a time when all friends seemed distant
seemed to have sailed away
and there in the mountains beyond the river
there was the silence of my own breath

was it a dream
or did you come to me in the night
slipping into that chilled room
like silver moonlight
falling through a window

and did you unwrap the scarves from your hair
and let fall that hair
and let fall the robes
that I have only seen since
in dusty cases that line the corridor

I felt the touch of your hand
a small hand
that had stained letters
with a brushed eloquence
and I lifted myself to hear your voice
and the voice of the golden crane
but the only sound was the echo of your steps
falling away into the past

4

for a moment I fight for breath
fight to remind myself
that it has been a thousand years
that I am alone in a room without light
that you are somewhere else
a part of memory
a part of some tattered painting
never seen
only imagined as I write this
pretending/wishing to be there
in the Poem-Chanting Tower
on the banks of the Brocade River
where willows make lace of the afternoon sun
and small bright birds
fly in at the open window
as you hold a hand to your mouth and laugh
at the letters that have just arrived
from an old poet

A LITTLE TOUCH OF TRUTH

I

if as you read this
you find
I rage like Lear and dare heaven
strike flat the thick rotundity of the world
will you laugh
at least grimace
squirm in your seat
and avoid the eye of your companion

and when I slip into a reverie
as I do
and find myself
watching butterflies that hover the willows
bright clouds of golden memories
reflected and doubled by the river
will you push back
into the unyielding slant of your chair
and glance impatiently at the hour

I indulge myself
slip on the robe my grandfather brought
as a gift from a surly empress
and watch the brush move through its paces
pulling ink into haunted shapes
I'll never understand

it's the way I pull these lines
out of the machine
out of the blankness of this screen
and the letters are gold and full of light
though with a flick of the finger
they disappear
the memory goes dead

11

as Xue Tao brushed a poem of tribute
for a dying scholar
at the far end of a yellow river
did she sometimes find herself lost
at the distractions of the afternoon
and let the brush slip and ink splatter

was it all gone
as a shout fell across the garden
and birds scattered into distant trees
and someone came to the steps
to ask about some indifferent matter

how can I
sitting here over a high caloric breakfast
in a diner where the waitress calls me 'hon'
or even here
in a high window
in the sun reflected from steel and glass
how can I
with any sense of truth
speak of you

you are the life that gives a lie
to the lie of these words

without you
without stumbling in the dark
as much toward you as toward this dream
of an ancient garden
on the banks of the Brocade River
there would be no sun
to fall through the window
and bring to these pages
a gleam of light
down which fall the moving letters of a life

see
I'll hang them here
beside the door

a thousand years ago
a beautiful woman sent them
down a thousand miles of the longest river
they arrived on the coldest day of spring
and brought a touch of the sun
to these distant mountains

A DANCE AT THE SHRINE

before the bronze mother
she dances alone
pushes body against a resistant stare
her hair oblique against the light
a reed at the edge of sleep
a dark dancing shift of a girl
lost to any effort I make
to catch her eye

she twists away
into a pale obeisance before the mother
and takes the gradual rain as if her right
while I make a dash for shelter
and turn to watch
as is my dry habit

she's no more now than a brush of ink
a calligraphic gesture
muted by rain and heaving of lungs

eyes without tears
full of rain that washes out the light
the bronze blind mother reaches
the girl rises into the gathering dark

she does not weep
she dances

she's only a child dancing in the rain
only a child

it's cold in my dry shelter

PORTRAIT

for Yü Hsüan-chi

she eats a storm cloud with her toast
and so by noon
must pour out words for anodyne

she hears the river's hiss and hush at night
and watches for the sun
to contradict the flow
to push against the moment

with words that break like ice
she paces light
the river's stir and stride
a path where voices from her childhood
trudge the mucky edges of the mind

with words that sound a distance
she never comes to rest
but seeks to flesh her coming in
with all the anguish at the bone

a lover writes from a distant town
'he is not wise or good'
she says
'it's just as well'

she bites another hunk of the world
chews and chokes and spits it out

I fake the scene of course
I met her once
and talked in a close corner of the room
distracted by the crush

her voice spilt words
cheap wine splashed the unraveling sleeve
bones prodded as words prod

there was a river in the falling voice
a sediment of possibilities

'she eats a storm cloud with her toast'
I thought
and so must pour out words or disappear

the moment passed
the party ended
she slipped back down the river's silent flank
to settle somewhere with a stir of words

ENCOUNTER IN THE GARDEN

the music was too loud
an assault on the rhythms of the night

we had left that room
and stood on steps above the garden
and spoke of poetry
and a different music that turns light
and cools the air

there in the midst of a harsh city
we spoke of the quiet gardens at Ch'ang-an
and the splash of a fountain
that was a continuing passage
down through valleys to a dark sea

our voices kept pace with the silence
while there at our backs
other voices rang harsh songs
on shrill laughter and drums

as she spoke of the death of a young poet
we watched a large cat wake
and step cautiously from a small grotto
step delicately among flowers
and stretching
rub the arc of his back against yellow blossoms

he turned at her whisper
and petals slipped from his fur
were caught by the wind
turned in a slow turning flight
and came to rest on the still moving water

the lights that had been fractured
by such a brief fall
were caught by her eyes
and for a moment sadness fell
with a small splash of laughter

she laughed again
lowered her eyes
and there were tears that glittered
gems of remarkable clarity

in that moment of silence
the very air of the garden filled with color
as an altar will flood with light

and there was that insistent drum
the harsh gaiety of other rooms
the ground on which this scene was drawn

nothing remarkable
an encounter on the edge of night
a brief exchange of words and silence
a vivid fall of color
a touching beyond all touching of the day

BRUSHING COLD FISHING NETS

the brush is often clumsy in my hand
reflecting an awkwardness of age
while reaching for the image
another poet might have felt

as Nukina Kaioku
not even Chinese
did or will one day do
with six panels of a Chinese poem
about brushing cold fishing nets

he splashes ink thickly
to write the following
down rolls of paper

*wild ducks fly far and waves stir the sand
as fishermen lower their nets*

*their small boat floats like grass
and they drift unable to see cold shrimp pass*

*however they pour out a massive catch of red-tailed carp
as the sleeves of their fishing coats flap*

*there's a frosty sound
and after the seines have sunk fully there's a perfect moon*

*they warm turtle-skin hands in a draft at the back of the brazier
which has matted fuel from half the bay*

*a gathering of reed blossoms
and the cold fishing nets by Nukina Kaioku*

even this title and this name
appear truncated with relief
down the last panel

and I am here
somewhere between then and now
trying to feel the flow of ink
the movement of thought in ink
a touch of passion in ink

I do not have the distance that it takes
I feel too bitterly the turtle-skin hands
that have come to me
a little more each year
with no brazier to warm them
as my words creep down the screen

perhaps a friend
who sings her song softly
in the gardens of the world
will unroll these words
and laugh with pleasure

YOUNG PAINTER

she crouches in the dim light
working within the fall of her own shadow

what light there might have been
is hooded
until she makes her slash across paper

we are unattended
by this dark flowing and awkward girl
whose fingers are stained with black
whose jawline holds a smear of gilt

I want to see what mark
she has left across her space
but she hovers
and pulls the surface into deeper shadow

the afternoon ends
and the master calls for scrolls to be hung
for painted poems to be read

with indifference
unaware of her own grace
she resists a pull of lights
the brittle inquisitive glances
the lift of superior smiles
and stands back
to sudden stillness

the room grows quiet
leaving only
quick steps of the master
a chattering of small bright birds

I stand pulling at breath
that will not come

great barred scrapes of gold and black
bite into the surface
and become the presence of the paint
the inky moment of the brush

this child
this girl
this woman
claws at our hearts
leaves us moved and baffled
silenced by some power in her presence
not there
until there
in the slash and lift of her brush

DEATH AND THE POET

at last
as his eyes sink through lost dreams

at last
as his face fades
into an indistinct sketch
and he no longer hides a preference
for color and lace
for two tall birds that ride his shoulders
and call defiance

at last
as his wife grows larger and more golden
flourishing
in the soft swing of her robes

at the last
I expect some revelation
something to encourage
something to console
some hint at the truth
that might lie at the heart
might lie to the heart
might have lain fallow
with a few weeds to cluster and clutter
and die again

at last
as in some abstract painting
he carries his own distortions
like some fabled heresiarch

he carries
not an owl or eagle of wisdom or strength
but two parrots
blue and gold and crimson in the flooding sun

two parrots
who speak not for food
but savagely in anger
slicing air with talon or beak

blue and gold and crimson in the sun
they drop their shit
in last tracings down his back

THE LAST VOYAGE

I

Wagner is appropriate for the highway
for rain and tears
and the pain of coming back

Tristan and Isolde hold each other
and die
as I cross the frontier
into that first valley
just west of K'uei-chou

it's where she always wanted to pause
where she always said
'it's really different'

and the rains stop
and I pull over to look again
at the greening valley

and know now
it is the last voyage that must be done alone

II

in spite of songs
an emperor had admired
during a winter evening while snow fell
I never seem to be quite there
except afterwards
when another poem brushes easily
across beautifully laid paper

with words like a fugue
that moves beyond its instrumentation
voice on voice
beyond our power to hear
over and over starting again

turning within the womb
of its own tumultuous birth

and so the painful trip
back to the mountains
to find it is not as I had expected

III

I had shared cries of discovery
moments of peering face to face
through crowded windows of childhood
at that hill and that old house
that valley falling toward the river
those three ridges rising toward the sun

but we cannot recover the edge
the shimmer of those early mornings
when mist lingers in the lower field
and deer
two then three and more
move silently through the hedge

the mill pond has been filled in
the stone house
where thirty years ago she wanted to live
has become an unprosperous shop
the woman who made beautiful pots
out of her despair
is dead

IV

three days to mourn
that's all
and then begins
the slow testing of the end

I had gone out in a soft rain
a bag of books and operatic tapes
maps and notes and linen
for an undetermined time

far from friends and the gardens at Ch'ang-an
I wait at the window
for the moon
for a continuing murmur of music

and in the darkness
always
that last great fugue
echoes still its own complexity
remains unresolved

DRAGON ROBE

I

the robe finally disappeared
the sword was ripped apart
by my brother
who wanted the coins for his collection

the elegant wooden boat
our grandfather had sailed upriver
to bring medication but little hope
to a dying queen and her people
was sold to pay his debts
to pay for the world he had used
to have the world he had wanted

it sat and faded
at an old pier
in a disintegrating harbor
where limp fishermen without teeth
for awhile remembered the elegant Doc
'who's long gone now'
they said
gone

2

soon after he died
the old house was falling to pieces
plaster shattered and drying
in corners of the room
and my ears full of warnings
not to notice
not to say a word
to sit straight and smile
at his aging sister
who really didn't care
who held her head high
and refused to see grindings of the world

no one really seemed to care
that he was gone
that he had wandered the globe
that he had been full of tales

no one really cared
that he was broken
forsaken by a wife who died
and never mentioned by his sons
never passed to another generation
the last of farm lands
sold for pine trees
that fought to survive

he left a sword
and a robe
already in a state of rot
and they disappeared
the things that held a final memory
gone

3

there were no letters that survived
no notebooks of a traveler
nothing that said
wait and I'll return

years later
he built the swing in a grapefruit tree
and gave me a push
and sighed a phrase or two
I never understood
but suspected even then
was a sigh fading from another world
to say how few of us will leave anything
that any one will care to remember

the old queen up that river in China
whispered to him in a language
he could only imitate
that the dragon on the robe
was to be taken and preserved
and given to someone who might fly again
who might rise into the future
with a cry
with a cry that might translate to
here I am
here's what we were really like
hold me
hold me close
and fly with me
fly with me higher than the moon

WAITING

I thought I had known what to expect
if not wisdom
then at least good manners
a comfortable chair in a frostless garden
only at a distance
the stale sweat of fear

a fog blots out the headland of spruce
a chill stalks the corridor
I light a fire
for your arrival
and hang an old lamp in the window

hardly have I turned toward the mirror
when I am struck
by whip scars that score my face

there's a moment
when the line of the jaw
goes slack

it is darker in the room
ashes smolder
chill persists
fog slouches and hovers the window
gathers itself at the door

will you come in such a darkness

I scratch these last fragments
unresolved
bristling with their own thorns

if you come
you will have to knock
very loudly

LETTER FROM EXILE

have you forgotten what it's like

the hours slide
through afternoons of heat and casual depression
the hours fall and die

under the whir and winnowing of strings
the sun is high
cicadas sound like fans

and still the strings ignore
the crumbling tower
the hour that seems to pass
between each breath

we sat beneath a dying elm
and talked
you and I
as strings wound their sound among stones
and dozed
where the tree left no fallen shadow

only the weight of the sun
could slow the hour
only a slide into silence
the cicadas's death

but still strings ignore the hour
the tower with its gaping wall retreats

I send these words to an old address

you'll know I meant them well
it's just an evocation
a sound cicadas make
before the shadow and the night
the silencing
and looming of the dark

it's such an old address
remember me

DYING FLOWERS FOR XUE TAO

as these flowers wilt
they carry in folded hearts
welcoming gestures
found in traces of your brush
that pay tribute to all guests

though these flowers wilt
in folded hearts they carry
the same rich gestures
that flow from a moving brush
of the poet you hold in awe

these wilting flowers
drop their petals and shrivel
but for a moment
they remind us of a brush
that moves black ink down these scrolls

lasting memories
welcome us as honored guests
like fragile flowers
like gestures that have been left
on scrolls that hang in your room

though nothing compares
with falling calligraphy
these brief flowers will
when they have dropped their petals
hold for us your memory

TWELVE MORNINGS

each morning for twelve mornings
I sat in this chair at this desk
and stared at some sooty structures
that line the horizon

until now
no line came
to smudge itself across the page
to claim the empty spaces for its own

until now
I heard only these strings
making melody from obvious scales
and dropping into the room
like sun
dropping unexpectedly through curtains

until now
I saw the distances grow in wordless wonder
a haunting
and there was no line that would cut
to that illusive contact
that only by accident can happen

what is there in the touching of this paper
to draw the silence
that settles from the corners of the room

how can I
listening to these strings
and taunted by the failure of words
by the failure of will
of good will
of caring
of love

how can I expect these lines
to speak
some sad and misunderstood and sooty thing
like truth

there were twelve mornings
during which I sat emptied of words
twelve mornings of blankness

that is one truth

and today there is another
I hear it in these strings
as they complete
somewhere in the undefined air of this room
the huge structure of their music
painfully
exultantly
defiantly

LANDSCAPE OF THE HEART

I

have you been up that road
there beyond the town
twisting among old men and dying cattle

you reach there by a way that is hard
and then harder

you stumble through an arroyo
slip across a scree
where mountains have crumbled into hills
and never come to rest

like coming home
only there is no home to come to

that too is the love of poetry
always there
and yet when I look again
back across one valley into another
it has turned to prose

II

the very earth flattens under the weight

a lingering light has been folded
into a darkness I can not comprehend

beyond these windows wind pulls a silence
that closes my heart
that pushes at stillness
that sings with the voice of a lost catamount

it was only a moment ago
the sun spilled
down blackened trunks
and earth was thick with the colors of death

only a moment before
and the skin of clouds
that by three were black and heavy
burst like ripe fruit over naked flesh

was it this morning
in the slow hour that bells the stirring day
a bird sang

I do not know why the room is so dark

III

why do we pass with such awkward gestures
our eyes stumbling like feet at the stone steps
our voices hesitant
swallowed in some painful memory
our shoulders haunted
by the weight and chills
that settle from the balcony
from the dark upper reaches of the room

where are the voices they promised us

they said we would hear
that somewhere
down that corridor or this
through that gate
past those great barred doors
voices would be like children in sunlight

outside
snow holds itself against branches
as if with some insatiable desire
holds and will not let go
until the sun
in its usual sign of passion
weakens the embrace

IV

the sky is neither full of clouds nor blue
with clarity of spring

one dead tree
lifts itself from the slow unfolding
seems centered
there beyond the window

I can not ignore its presence
I look away
give attention to doves lifting themselves
awkwardly against waves of wind
note vagaries of distant houses
white and clean with illusions of morning light

but I come back
my eyes resigned to that centered tree
bare limbs that resist the movement of wind

they break and shatter under snow
against the drift
dry and lighten
through drought of summer
until their presence
carried by no memory but these words
grows dim on the brittle page

v

a moment only
to touch and move on
that's all

we gather luggage and slowly settle
for a wait
a read
we try not to panic
we let go and drift away
under the rattle of voices

we know that there will be plenty of time
next week
to say what was never so clearly said
to do what is unremembered

but then
tomorrow I'll look it up
make a list

I'll remember then
and then sing
then love
then see

that's it
plenty of time
to avoid the silence that slips over us
softly
like a silk shroud

VI

the waters of the bay lie flat
reflect only the gray remains of day
the slight rise spreads
and falls back
surprises by reluctance

the cry of a gull
muted
restrains

the cries of children
no longer shrill with continuance
hover the edge

at such a moment
beside these waters
spindrift's a gentle memory
anticipation more gritty than gray sand

with suddenness
in silence as palpable as water
our bodies shatter beyond light
absorbed by untouched folds of the moment

there and not there
we are receiving fragments of the stars
and then not even that

TU FU'S VOYAGE OF FAREWELL

I

he should have been renewed by the voyage
should have been off on another adventure
except that he was tired
he was old

it was not a time for contemplation of ships
it was a time to breathe deeply
within the rounded gate of his garden
instead
he was on a dusty road
pushing from one village to another

when the world fell apart
and tranquility rotted
in hearts he thought would last
he made the painful trip back to the mountains
and found it was not as he had expected

he was not the sort to have said he had fucked up
but in spite of poems
that even an emperor
had admired on quiet winter evenings
he wept

2

down to the curb
for embarkation in a slow rain
with books and scores and identification papers
that might never be needed
maps and notes for an undetermined time

even as he packed
he remembered pens and pills
and swore he'd leave the pain and disappointment

how far can one go in a lifetime
in a day
when at the end of the day
when sun drops
and night comes suddenly
so dark
one hill becomes another
becomes sky
and only feet
stumbling down a path
toward a place where one might rest
make a distinction between up and down

3

only occasionally now
in sudden silence away from traffic
he hears in old streets
a woman's laughter
fall from upper balconies
through strips of curtain
falling slowly in summer's heat

on any street wider than an alley
fumes of a crowd
are too heavy for him to sit outside

back alleys and a narrow walkway
are full of small restaurants
where the food is good
with a taste he has only known elsewhere

4

can one go back
can one recover the edge and shimmer
of those early mornings
when mist lingered in the lower fields
and she rose to wait for the sun
and hummed a song barely remembered

now he is at the edge of a valley
that stretches south over distant ridges
like six lutes in the ricercar
that has heralded his arrival in this place

the sun is warmer
than it has been

5

he had not known it would become a voyage of farewell
even the fugues stretched beyond their instrumentation
voice on voice beyond his power to hear
over and over
starting again
turning within and over
beyond whatever lay beneath

he could not decide whether he wept
for music that buried itself within his ears
his chest
his heart
or if his skin were vibrating with the sound
and he was the music
as he was the hill and the road he trudged

I am this path that drops through woods
he says aloud to no one

I know the pond it passes
I have swum there toward a setting sun
in those moments when we saw
together
what the world might be
what we might become

6

when he stopped at an inn to be refreshed
were the shrimp fresh from the river
was the wine brought cool to the table
were other diners indifferent to his presence
did he sit there
a poet grown old and tired
who still could not resist
placing a notebook beside his cup of wine

he always stayed at the best inns
where as it grew late
the tables filled with men
he might have known at court

in the shadow of those almost forgotten mountains
he ate well and sat late with a cup of the best
though he was not sure whether he knew them
the couple at the next table
familiar neighbors
or figures from one of his own poems
or that man too young to have been important
yet with a companion
a wife
a woman of class
a subject for a painting by a courtly scribe

7

a two-day voyage ended at a bar with too much wine
and too many tears
memories he thought were gone
flushed by violence of another war

she had gone another route he could not know
he could not share
not even his daughters
whatever their way
could share his way

however much he might wish for that touch
he was alone
here at the bar of this distant inn
drinking a local wine she might have enjoyed

it was a bar that wasn't here when they were here
though the room was
and the chairs and the mirror
as part of a past they had shared briefly

she was somewhere else
he didn't know where
and their daughters had become women
with their own integrity
their own space to explore

we were so sure
he says almost aloud to no one
we were so sure we had preserved our own space
and protected the space of the other

his glass was empty
it was her town
her schools
her relatives
and she wasn't here
he was alone
he no longer knew anyone in the village
where so much had begun
where they had shared cries of discovery
and moments of peering face to face
into crowded windows of her childhood

perhaps it was an intrusion into her world
and yet she had made him a part of what she was
and it had become his world
that hill
that village down the Yangtse
over Lake Tung-t'ing and up the Hsiang River
he thought it would be a grand homecoming
a return for reassurances

from the moment he approached the first valley
just west of Ch'ang-an
a place she always wanted to stop
where she always said it's really different
the rains stopped
as he paused beneath a pine
to look once again
out over the greening valley
and knew that this had become
his voyage of farewell

8

behind the opaque window
there is a poem of sorts
of all sorts
of the crisis in a mystery half heard
as the body presses awake
and the eye can't see
but voices insist
and a cry almost suppressed
forces silence
and the poem waits
unseen beyond the painted frame

if he could find it
that poem
before the word has fixed it to the page
has forced a shape
while it's a cry almost heard at twilight
there beyond the window
through which he cannot see
then what
a truth
the mystery explained
or just another fiddling with despair

he was never sure if this was only
a pattern of lonely panic
words that scatter sound across an empty room
and pull him from sleep
pull him once again through the light of anguish

there is no resolution through opaque windows
only doubt
and the muffled echo of a dream

9

the old generation was gone
he had not known they would live so long
like frail insects stirring against last light
he had watched them die slowly
a little more each day
a staring eye distracted only by a touch
a hand fighting against the rising of a spoon
against unwanted food

he wanted to give them his permission to go
he wanted to say
yes you may die
don't wait for us
don't wait on us
you've always waited for us to finish
and now we wait for you to finish
you've always waited for us to call goodbye
as we ran from the door eager and indifferent
it's all right
go go

and now over wine in this distant inn
he remembers his father saying it's hot
not knowing where to hold
to pull or pant or punch
to relieve the pain
he had watched his father's eyes turn red
and blaze for a moment
with defiance
but it was short lived

never defeated by life
he was finally defeated by age and pain
as he waited to die

but who was I to say that he might go
I would not say stay
I could not say go
I could only wait and watch
the incredible loneliness of the end
for he who had never been alone

there was an awful slowness to that time
when every sound was magnified
a wheeze and rumbling from the kitchen
a clatter from the distant stable
at the back of the house

however old that house
it seemed to settle and creak
not year by year
but day by day
with the scurry of insects or mice
among papers on his desk

'what time is it' he would suddenly ask
with a sigh and a blurred turning toward the window
every ten minutes or an hour or a day
with hardly a difference
except for potions that did no good
a green one on the hour
a red one with uneaten meals

they die we all die
or we don't die
we linger in pain and silence
and the indifference of the world

it was different then he thought
we cared
we lingered beside the bed and waited

he lifted his cup of wine to the empty room
war or pestilence would have given
some meaning to their death
he thought
this silent antiseptic waiting
is a cruel laughless joke of heaven

10

*sometime later
wandering further from the fringes of power
he would send this poem
from the green mountain inn*

there's a moment
when the line of the jaw goes soft
three days to mourn
three days
that's enough and then it begins

how many days down river
into another lifetime of mourning

one is never quite there
except years afterwards
when the poem brushes easily
down an especially stretched piece of silk

with moments of a faulty memory
moments that count
verbal moments
in the splash of ink

AFTERNOON ON THE BROCADE RIVER

shirt open
lying warm in a river pavilion
we chant poems aloud
about the rustic scene

as water flows
and my heart ceases to struggle
the clouds are here
my mind as calm as they
                —*Tu Fu*

the Brocade River is shallow and cool
except where it rolls rocks into piles
thrust out and warmed in summer sun
that give us a place where
as children splash
we chant poems
and share a dream about shattering dreams
and rebuilding lives
already lost so many times

how pleased I was he liked words
I'd found in earlier hours of the day
about Mozart and Purcell
before I'd heard them where he said one should
'in the dark of a high cathedral'
or falling from a tower

as he was dying
he still remembered
that we lay naked in the sun all afternoon
wondering if we would ever find
the calmness of clouds that gathered color
as night came slipping down river
through reborn woods
and made it seem a place of rustic lingerings

later we wandered cities searching
for what was there
right there that afternoon
with children unaware of what lay ahead
and with our own anticipations
that brought a chill to the heart

it's been a long time
and names and rivers change
and the chanting of poems
has become too formal a thing

he made a name
and I
well 'to drive off sadness
I make myself write poems'

but that's a line he wrote
with an unsteady hand
a line he scratched
while on the banks of a river
one more line
to reach back to a distant past

and then he died
before I could share books
I'd spent many years trying to make right
for an afternoon
when the sound of their words
might drift through branches
of 'woods back home'

EIGHT FAMOUS DRINKERS

Tu Fu wrote the original poem
or copied one that was known
long before I moved to the Ompompanusic River
where Ned and I chilled bottles of wine in shallows
while arguing about what music
should drift from the shack
to make cheap wine taste better

the first to arrive for an afternoon party
was always John Chang
sitting on an old farm horse as if riding a boat
eyes glazed and rolling
with those banal poems he liked to chant
until he would stumble into the shallow well
and sleep there until dinner

then Joe Yang wandered about bragging
of the three gallons he needed before going to court
and broke out salivating
at the memory of a cart-load of wine-yeast
he had seen on the road
and regretted that he had never been transferred
to a post in the wine country

meanwhile Tom Hanks staggered about
drinking like a whale swallowing a hundred streams at once
to support his happiness
bragging that he had spent all his inheritance
ten thousand a day
and now loves only the wise
and can do without the worthy

everyone stopped for a moment to watch the Hugh boy
join us on the river
a handsome free and easy kid
weaving a bit
who lifted his cup and gazed at blue skies
with the whites of his eyes
and sparkled like a jade tree facing a brisk wind

in real contrast Surry Chin walked about
with great solemnity and bowed to each of us
before he set up an embroidered Buddha
in front of whom he fasted
in spite of gay music that drifted about
for once he's drunk
he loves just to sit and meditate

then Lee Poe
who after a single drink will write a hundred poems
and fall asleep in a wine shop down river
arrived late with an excuse
that heavenly voices had summoned him
since he was as we should know
an immortal of the wine

Chuck Sue after drinking three cups
showed his work as master of cursive calligraphy
wielding his brush across paper
like mist or clouds that drift
until with enthusiasm he threw off his cap
and exposed his bald pate
right in front of all of us

finally Joe Shoer
after an hour of silence
and five dippers of our best cheap wine
came to life and stumbled upright
and with a noble discourse and earthy lecture
startled us all into laughter
with words only famous drinkers can inspire

(based on a poem by Tu Fu)

ORCHID PAVILION

There's a famous scroll at the museum
that I've enjoyed looking at
as its calligraphy moves across the page
like a corps of dancers at their best
(though it translates like a piece of academic shit)

it starts as if it were from my own memories
of the end of a distant decade
on the Ompompanusic River
when year-rounders and summer-folk
gathered for a party at the Orchid Pavilion
on Hubbard Hill in Thetford Center
(except that the pavilion for orchids
I watch closely
didn't exist for another 40 years)

Thetford is an area of low mountainous humps
above luxuriant woods with a few lingering elms
and streams and rapids that glitter like jade belts
(one of the few good lines by Wang Hsi-chih
who wrote this famous preface
for a collection of poems that did not survive)
where Ned and I often chilled cheap wine
for guests stretched out on the banks
waiting their turn to chant a poem

as I gaze on the scroll
all of this lines up with my own memories
up through space beyond clouds
and down
to watch myriad little critters crawl
among leaves that will soon become summer wheat
(and yes
our eyes explore and our minds race
even before we start on the wine)

now as I look back at this Orchid Pavilion scroll
I become confused
am I looking at something that is famous
for the way ink flows down the page
or is there a poem hidden
somewhere in the painter's sense of sight and sound

he says he wants
to give joy that endures a lifetime
whether we are shoulder to shoulder with other people
in rooms that draw upon the heart and mind
or stretched in pavilions open to the outside world
buffeted by unrestrained happiness
as we had hoped to be that afternoon
down on the rocks of the Ompompanusic

then something curious happens
somewhere between an old poet's
concept of a quiet breeze and a rowdy clap of thunder
when not even an academic translation
can find the line
except with a sigh

when one is exhilarated by something
even if it is ever so fleeting
one feels satisfied and forgets
that old age lurks just ahead
and that pleasure is the balance we seek
while our short lives are in constant flux

who is this painter-poet
lamenting that past pleasures
have become mere traces in history
who is pained even to think
that birth and death might be
the two grimmest events of life

he seems upset (though sensible)
and says he can not agree with ancient poets
who may have been his guests
at the Orchid Pavilion that summer afternoon
when he read their writings
though he could not share their feelings

but then he makes a clearer point
(at least it seems to be his point)
and I'm left wondering how far calligraphy stretches
as it stretches here to me
in a copy attached to an email
from a friend at the museum

will people of the future look back at us
he says
and is that the equivalent of our looking back
to our own ancestors

so I have no choice but to pay attention
to my contemporaries and record their words
as I've recorded here my own struggle
to find what those gathered on that clear afternoon
might have shared
of what's held by the ink
of what flows with the ink

(based on a translation of Wang Hsi-chih)

CHINESE SCHOLAR'S STUDY

I

from a high floor over roof tops
to the horizon
and a ship that slowly disappears
beyond a bridge that takes
this world to somewhere I can't see
not from here

or from the edge of a lagoon
across sea grass and sails
to a horizon that glitters with sun
and disappears into a part of the sky
beyond which again I can not see

or here in a room
across piles of books and Buddhas
and down the hall
across old rugs
to a black piano
that will carry me to a world
beyond sheets of music

are the places I've lived
that have helped me see
have given shelter
from demands of the street
and a place to stretch words
as if on a piece of silk

2

I've never lived among cliffs or valleys
or followed a path
where wanderers search for something new
or move
just move among ruins of another time
a lost time

I've wanted to
I've wanted to follow ancient routes
through steppes of central Asia
and written poems about those who did
and read books of those who did

and yes
I've climbed a pyramid or two
and heard voices in deserted villages
now almost dust
and stood on walls
where stones slowly fade from memory

but always with the safe retreat of a shower
wine and service with a smile
no echo of the drums and angry cry
that could at any moment mean death

3

it's too much like the world of a Chinese scholar
this world of mine
a scattering of fine calligraphy
a smiling Buddha and a stone where dragons dwell
like the one preserved in the local museum
a fine place to visit
but who would want to live there

and yet I do
and would not now live in another place

a few gnarled trees with twisted branches
scrape against the window
fragrant herbs flourish
just at the back door
ready for adding to a soup
and in the comfort of where I live
I've learned to smile and make a song
even if my calligraphy
flows down the screen of an efficient computer

DREAM LANTERNS

three lanterns light an early morning dream
or is it one taking over with a glare

I reach from my pillow
into the list of a dream
and find myself for a moment disoriented
not sure which way is up
which way down

they often appear
about the time sun breaks through trees
at the bottom of the field

if the field is real
I tell myself
the lantern must be real
for I can reach and touch and feel fired clay
as it cools

the woods can not be touched
they're somewhere else
on the edge of complications
or simply hiding a vineyard
where a dream may start or end

the nature of my dream can be so real
I think for days
I really search for lanterns
and perhaps I do

I lie in bed growing older
as I lie awake watching the sky
grow light
through open windows beyond the sheets

and see I say as if aloud
the lanterns have the calligraphic mark
of a famous potter

but why
over and over
do these lanterns light

is it a need to stay in touch with the world
is it part of the liturgy the world has used
to show us that the sun will rise again
that light will flood the corners of our life

it's I who lights the lantern
even in a dream
even in that precarious balance
when all alone we light the lamp
and laugh at what we've finally learned
to do ourselves
if only by manipulating dreams

AUTUMN COMES

somewhere in the tangle
of a dead aunt's rotting possessions
my mother found an old Chinese fan
which she slipped into the back of a drawer
with sweet boxes of fine powder

it must have been special
she said before she died
it may have been one of our grandfather's pieces
most of which disappeared

I had never seen it before
and even though it was more frail each year
I too stuck it in the back of a drawer
until years later
an old Chinese friend and I
pulled it out
and tried to make a translation

there was something there
some hint of catastrophe
that made it immediately appealing

somewhere to the left of the fan
just before the poetry stops
someone says
the poet says
a lover whispers
'please don't lean on the railing
that can only add pain to grief'

otherwise
it's just an autumnal poem
with the clear colors of a river town
blue-green willows
and loud chirping of cicadas
as mist rises and sun sets
lighting for one last moment red lotus petals

it must be she
who approaches despair
for the poet says she is aging
with grey hair and withered skin
as in her desolation
she stares out
at falling darkness
the falling of another year

perhaps it's she who at that moment
leans against the railing
of the small pavilion
and pushes toward a setting sun
not wanting to wait for later years

all this
all this on a beautiful fan that has survived
that has passed from generations down
that has carried the memory of their love

*(based on a fan with calligraphy by Wen Cheng-ming
seen on the cover of this book)*

TEN CONVENIENCES

friends from town made fun of us
when we patched together our rakes and books
and moved to a house
on a mountain beyond the city
and closed our gate to the world

and though we acted
as if we'd lost all connection with that world
even to the point of brushing aside
any tracks that might linger on the path
occasionally an old friend would appear

it's amazing one guest said
that you've achieved such serenity
but how can you overcome the inconveniences
and make a living
this far removed from the masses

I had to demonstrate with a set of poems
with a set of ten conveniences how off the mark he was
given a natural profit of mountain and stream
and a natural privacy of thought
encouraged by piles of books and hours of silence

1 - Convenient For Chanting Poems

from right here where my window shutters open
almost as if by accident
I look out on a gorgeous mountain view
so that I need not go in search of poems
for poems come here as if by themselves

don't marvel that my purse is empty
I'm rich in verse and poems that emerge
that have only come into being
since I've been living here
in this little creative paradise

2 - Convenient For Fishing

to fish I need no bamboo hat
no raincoat
and I never could stand to ride in a boat
each day I just sit out here on the east porch
and learn to throw a net for tortoise

visitors always bring wine
and we sit here and leisurely toss sweet bait
down over the railing
and pull out enough small fish
for a lovely meal

3 - Convenient For Planting

to protect the rich green
of these mountain fields
that lie just outside the bramble gate
there's the river
that bends and gathers right there

and if by noon the roosters
no longer disturb the day
we farmers eat lunch
as we work the fields
with no need of wives to bring food

4 - Convenient For Irrigating The Garden

and see how we've built a little garden here
beside the square-shaped pond
where it's easy for fruit to grow
and vegetables as well
almost anything you'd want to eat

lugging water jars
would be too stupid and too refined a technique
our method is simply to scoop water
from the pond with whatever's at hand
and pour it right into the beds

5 - Convenient For Drawing Water

with the splashing of a mountain stream
just beyond the wall of our mountain kitchen
it takes little more than a single pipe
with a sensible carved bamboo tip
to bring inside a never-ending stream

so right away
when a fine guest arrives
like the one for whom I write these conveniences
we brew tea that carries a natural flavor
of stones from an ancient source

6 - Convenient For Supervising The Farmers

my mountain windows look out
from all four sides with perfect clarity
as green fields out there and rice paddies there
fall into a pattern
right before my eyes

so with my elbows propped on my desk
I can supervise farmers and gardeners
all day
and it never interferes
with the important job of reading books

7 - Convenient For Gazing

though our old shepherd yells at his sheep
from inside his cave of immortals
his pair of eyes and mine too
will make in a single day
several sightseeing trips

but since even then he has not
he says
achieved a vision of a thousand miles
he escorts the clouds as they scud
far above the peaks of Mount Kua-ts'ang

8 - Convenient For Washing

there's no need to wander down stream
to wash off dust and grime
waters that flow inside the gate
are exceptionally pure
clear and enticing

it's not that as a hermit
I'm obsessed with perfect cleanliness
but the clarity of the currents
suddenly makes me want to wash
even the dirty strings of my work cap

9 - Convenient For Gathering Wood

lots of extra help comes
and stays busy during the growing season
gathering branches to warm the winter
and sweeping off leaves
to fill the forest with rich mulch

/ *91*

it's a time when I must put aside my books
and luckily go out to check
what Lalo and Beth are up to
for just as I scramble out the bramble gate
there! there are the mountains

10 - CONVENIENT FOR GUARDING AT NIGHT

it may be just a simple house
beyond the coldness of the local village
lonely and desolate
but all we need is the gushing stream
to guard at night the bramble gate

we pull the drawbridge
to cut off the pathway at twilight
so even the mountain dog
sleeps soundly
by the roots of an ancient tree

(based on 'Ten Conveniences of the Garden of Yi'
with preface by Li Yü and painted by Taiga at Ku-Zu)

FOR TS'ANG CHIEH

when his brush lifted
for the first time
having left a trail of slashes
that spilled toward the bottom of the page
having left an order of sound
words
that leave a mark upon memory

the earth trembled
clouds broke apart
spilled dark tears across low hills

rice flourished
and workers
returning from a field
sang the very song that lingers
still on this scroll
that graces the wall of my study

in a city so far removed
that when I trace unknown letters
and let my fingers touch silk
that has lasted a thousand years
I leave smudges of soot
and ash from a thousand graves

COLD-MOUNTAIN POEM

before answering
I'll let this letter sit on the screen
where it can quickly remind me
be brought to light again
and nourish me
in the way an empty envelope would nourish
as I try to decide
if you're deliberately coy
or there's pain from
which your words have fallen

Cold-Mountain people try to laugh
look up an old routine
and polish it for the table
like the old pot I polished for cheap soup
on nights colleagues came to celebrate
the chanting of poems
it never made the soup
taste better
but Han Shan could not have cared

Nor did George
when pushing strings to the edge
try to laugh or drop the pain he felt
onto another instrument

just look at this
I try to write a letter
that thanks you for reminders of Cold Mountain
and find myself pushing words into piles

I drop what I am doing
and limp downstairs to find Han Shan
and find him in the center
of a wall of books

but wait I tell myself
something's wrong
as if the poems had been left
rotting under needles of red pines in the fall

this one doesn't move the way it should
it doesn't move the way you quote it moving
the way I remember it moving
which means you had better be careful
or I'll curse you for pulling me in
for getting me started again
now that the tribute for Xue Tao is finished
and I must find a better route
to the Cold Mountain
when I thought it was time for rest beside a fire

I thought you and I
were ready to explore the pain
find images that just might work
just might pull a salve over scars
our lives have gathered
the ones we try to deny
as images appear on paper we've chosen
for someone else
to share as with a laugh

BUDDHA'S SERMON AT LU ZHAI

the mountains seem empty of people
except for their voices in an echo
that falls like sunlight through deep forests
and glitters across the top of black lichen

(20th version of a poem by Wang Wei)

This bit of calligraphy from the fan says 'Lovely One.'

POEM OF AUTUMN
A Modified Translation

it happened down in the river village
when autumn colors were clear and passionate
and blue-green willows
and chirping cicadas
were locked in a sweep of mist

something of a tropical moment
when new coolness generated songs
as simple and elegant as folded white linen
brought a night of rain there on the west lake
and red lotus petals down in a flurry

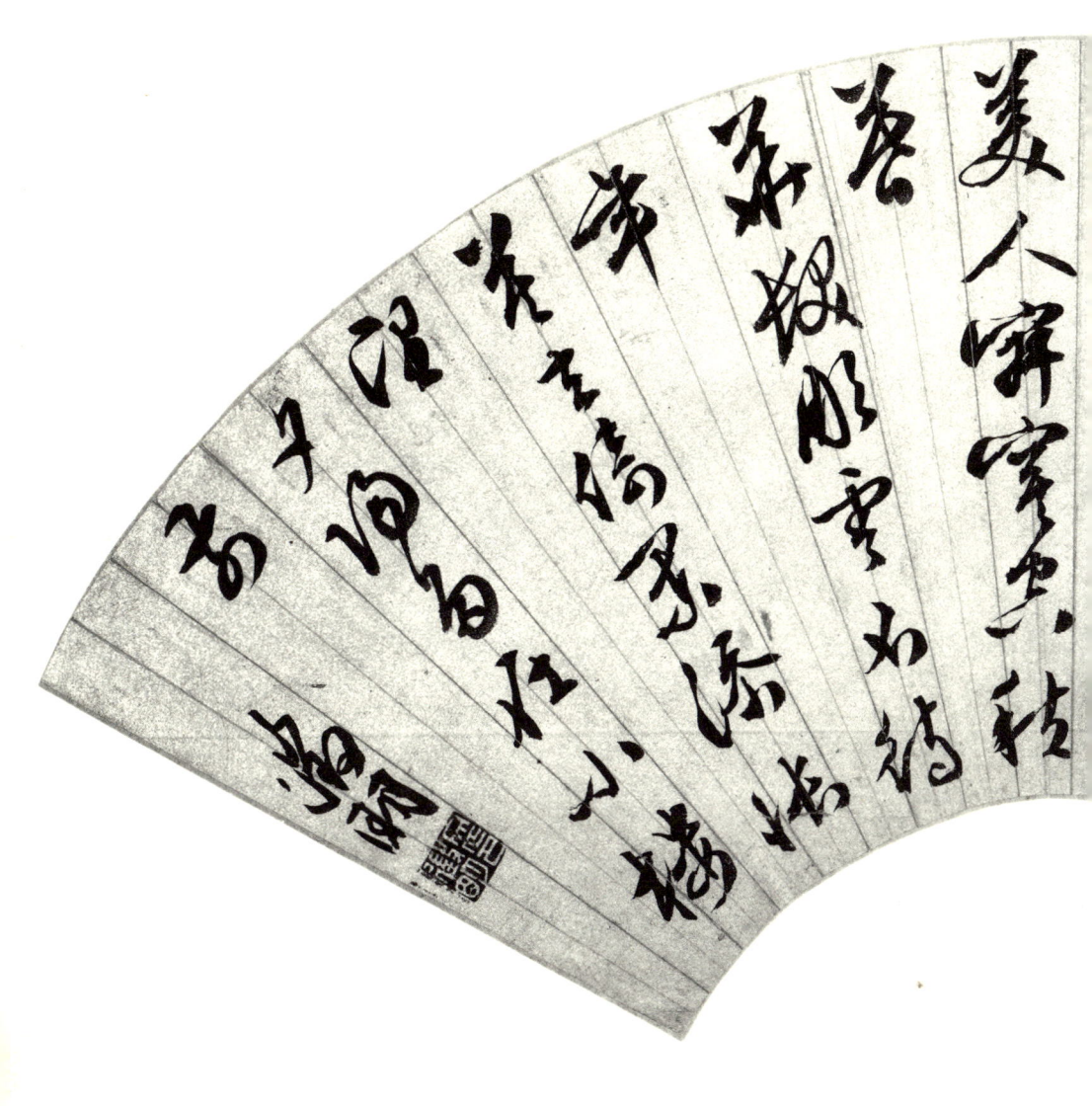

*his lovely one had become desolate
and in vain grieved at the blustery evening
when her gray hair
seemed to be withering too soon
for someone still too young to feel so faded*

*her lover murmured with tenderness
please don't lean upon the railing
for that can only add pain to grief
and the sun set rapidly
right there beyond the small pavilion*

Wen Cheng-ming (1470-1559)

BIOGRAPHICAL NOTE FOR WILLIAM HOLLIS

He listened in on a strange adult world as he grew up in central Florida during the thirties and, with his grandfather's help, started to write poems. And since he was one of the few kids who played the piano well, he had a wonderful opportunity to overhear women in Winter Haven and Lake Wales and men in Tampa and Orlando talk about the whispered sides of their lives. He would play Liszt after a luncheon and rush home to write a poem about some slick man with polished nails or the woman who hissed that she never wore underwear.

During college at W&L and Princeton, where he could never tie himself to one major, and during a year in Europe on a Fulbright, he was a loner, trying to find ways to make verbal music out of observed human experience. He sat on mountain tops and listened to an echo of voices, slept in cheap youth hostels, fell in love with Australian girls and the Grand Canal in Venice, ate in the cheapest White-Russian cafés, and tried to write poems more up-to-date than Keats. And then, after the army, he hit thirty, married, taught at Dartmouth and Drexel, had a family, two daughters, and found that poetry had to be relegated to summer vacations. The poems kept coming anyway, even after he grew tired of trying to fit into 'the literary scene,' a scene that never worked for him except when reading in bars and bookshops of Philadelphia.

Photo: Andrea Baldeck

At 50, retired from teaching, unhappy with life, divorced, trying to be a painter or a musician, which he found he wasn't, he still wrote, volume after volume, as the world turned around, in spite of stupid wars of power and greed, and poems came with more frequency and he met and married a wonderful musician/physician/photographer, Andrea Baldeck, who peered out at the world with as much curiosity as he; and they went places where they could explore their own possibilities in their art. They spent several winters on a strange little island called

Carriacou where the food was bad and the wine terrible, but the people warm and accepting; they spent several springs and autumns on Cumberland Island, off the coast of Georgia, or Vieques, watching people and gulls and the crashing of waves. And then, following a hunger they had both had since youth, they rented and furnished a flat on the Grand Canal in Venice, where they lived half the time for a number of years. Many poems in his *Dark Encounter in Mid Air* and photographs in her *Venice a personal View* were created in the windows of that apartment as they watched boats and waved to tourists and hugged their way into dozens of friendships.

They continue to have a life outside of Philadelphia, surrounded by gardens and great piles of books and a growing collection of art that's primarily local or East Asian. But their days are mostly filled with work. Her photographs and his poems are a continuing manifestation of collaboration, as well as the result of what they have seen out there in the crazy world. The poems are still his; the photographs hers—but the work is something they hope will move readers or viewers as only music, images, verbal rhythms, and felt ideas can. As she works on *Buddhist Himalaya*, her next book, he has discovered Lilith and remembered the tortured blues from the cotton fields of Georgia for a volume to be called *Lilith and the Blues* that should follow soon after *Poem-Chanting Tower*.

Every day is a day for working with enthusiasm.

BOOKS BY WILLIAM HOLLIS

A Collection of Early Encounters

Letters And Voices From The Steppes

Midlife Encounters

Sketches For A Mayan Odyssey

Scenes From An Old Album

Sonata Sonnets

Las Espinas

Letter Poems

Venetian Variations

Dark Encounter In Mid Air

Poem-Chanting Tower

Design and production of this book were managed by
Veronica Miller & Associates, Haverford, Pennsylvania.
Production supervision was provided by Peter Philbin.
The book was printed by Brilliant Graphics, Exton, Pennsylvania
and was bound by Hoster Book Bindery, Ivyland, Pennsylvania.